A Girl's Rules for Life, Plus a Golden Rule

From Your Mother Who Loves You

Stacie Davies

Copyright © 2016 Stacie Davies

All rights reserved.

ISBN: 1530880380
ISBN-13: 978-1534880382

Cover art © 2016 Stacie Davies

STACIE DAVIES

All My Best,

Stacie Davies

Dedicated to my daughter.

STACIEDAVIES.LIFETOPICS

Dear Young Lady,

Life does not come with a rule book or a set of instructions. There are no manuals leading us through the awkward teen years, relationships, or parenting for that matter. There are plenty of self-help books out there, and they can be very helpful, but they are not often simple. This little book of rules is just that, simple. It's filled with thoughts and ideas to help guide you through the sticky situations in life and possibly even help you avoid the sticky situations all together. Keep in mind as you read, these rules are <u>merely suggestions</u> coming from someone who has been there. Most of these suggestions were presented to me while I was growing up; some from my mom, some from my grandmother, and a large portion came from my dad. My dad knew everything! For real.
Some rules are funny and some rules are serious but they all are very useful.

As I have lived my life, I have witnessed these situations over and over. I have seen the writing on the wall. I have heard the boys talk and I have watched great ones fall and meager ones rise. I do not claim perfection as I have broken some of the rules myself, but I've tried to learn from my every mistake and the mistakes of those I love. In life, we are always experiencing new things. We go through one experience and blend right into another. Ride the wave and learn from it. It's fun.

Suggestions for Positive Living

Rule #1
You do not need 1,000,000 friends, you need four: a wise friend, a trustworthy friend, an honest friend, and an old friend.

Rule #2
In reference to Rule #1, you can actually have only one friend, provided they have all four qualities.

Rule #3
Never date a guy who has a butt, which is smaller than yours, especially if he makes notice of this.

Rule #4
Be very wary of men in vans…no, not the shoes, the vehicle.

Rule #5
You will not get ahead in life by hanging out at the mall. Malls are for shopping. Don't be a mall rat.

Rule #6
Never write anything down that you don't want to come back and bite you in the ass, because it will. Never fails. Texts count.

Rule #7
Go to the bathroom before you go to the bar and wait to go again until you come home. Bathrooms in bars are for barfing, doing drugs, smoking cigarettes, and generally naughty activity. Do not get caught in the bathroom of a bar.

Rule #8
Never take photos of yourself or video yourself doing something you'll be judged for. Same theory of Rule #6 applies. It will come back and bite you.

Rule #9
If someone else wants to take a photo or video of you doing something questionable, leave the situation immediately. It's going to escalate quickly and not end well.

Rule #10
Everyone will remember what you did in high school. Good and bad, but mostly bad.

A GIRL'S RULES FOR LIFE, PLUS A GOLDEN RULE

Rule #11
No one will remember what you did in college. Unless you dropout and don't graduate. Everyone remembers that.

Rule #12
Reduce, reuse and recycle, but don't be a hippie about it. Just do it out of respect for the Earth and future generations.

Rule #13
Don't swear unless you really mean it. Ladies who curse in their day-to-day vocabulary are not ladies but rather women who have foul mouths. Swearing has a purpose, use it wisely. When you are mature and a parent, you may curse, respectfully of course and never in front of your children.

Rule #14
Never flip someone the finger in your own hometown, especially if it's a small town. Chances are the person you just flipped off is the principal at your future child's school.

Rule #15
Never drive or operate a vehicle of any kind under the influence of anything impairing. You will have a wreck, get pulled over & thrown in jail, or worse yet, kill someone. This has been proven over and over again, but stupid people keep doing it.

Rule #16
Don't smoke. If this actually need explaining, I feel bad for you…good luck.

Rule #17
Treat your body like a Porsche (or your favorite, 6 digit, exotic, sports car) feed it the best food, keep air in the tires and most certainly do not park next to junkers! BTW – you wouldn't let just anyone drive your Porsche, now would you? Be wise.

Rule #18
Learn to cook something other than spaghetti and Top Ramen. Being a chef-of-sorts is a very handy and respectful skill.

Rule #19
Do not behave like a raunchy street-walker. If you behave in such a way, you are simply that.

Rule #20
Do not dress like a raunchy street-walker. Same theory applies as Rule #19.

Rule #21
Trust no one, until they give you at least three, significantly good reasons to trust them. This is sad, but realistic and true. Never trust first and ask questions later. That's backwards.

Rule #22
Although our judicial system says otherwise, men are generally guilty until proven innocent. One of my favorite male expressions of all time, "deny it till you die." Enough said.

Rule #23
Do not fall into the trap of constantly needing validation from others. Be confidant in yourself without needing others to tell you that you look nice, that you're smart, that you're a pleasant person or whatever the case may be. Be proud of yourself.

Rule #24
Do your best to not have "C" taste in music. Explore classical, oldies, reggae, rock and roll, jazz, indie and more. Don't just listen to the crummy music on "Hits." Generally speaking, it's trash and has no real musical value. The lyrics are trashy and the riffs are simplistic. Music that crosses generations will always be respected and remembered. Most of the music on "Hits," will not.

Rule #25
Do not be ordinary, be unique, be you. Everyone is ordinary and trying to look just like, dress just like and drive the same car as the next person, be yourself and choose what YOU like.

Rule #26
Learn a foreign language. I can't stress this enough! Try to

choose a language, which will be useful for the future, but none-the-less, learn one.

Rule #27
Be accountable. Always!

Rule #28
Don't blame others. When you blame others for something you did, you sound like a fool.

Rule #29
Have expectations only for yourself, not for your parents, siblings, friends or associates. Having expectations for others is setting yourself up for a huge disappointment. Every time.

Rule #30
Set goals for yourself, annually.

Rule #31
Bad choices lead to bad consequences, natural or otherwise. Bad choices are simply that, bad and they never end up with good results.

Rule #32
Do not judge or be judgmental of other's weight, looks, financial status, clothing, handbags, hairstyles, job or professional status, vehicle, home address, among other things. If you don't like someone, for whatever reason, walk away. Don't judge, just walk away. Your judgment

of them means nothing and no one really cares what you think anyway. You just end up sounding like a spoiled brat.

Rule #33
If you do not like someone's behavior or lifestyle, or those things about a person bother you, just turn away and go on about your business. No one gets hurt.

Rule #34
Never attempt to change or fix a person. This does not happen and it is only a frustrating lesson in futility. This has never worked and never will.

Rule #35
If you must drink alcohol, use control and have only one drink. Drink slowly. If you feel like you "need" another drink, there is a good chance that danger is lurking in your future. Drinking may not be for you.

Rule #36
If you do choose to consume alcoholic beverages, do not ever drink cheap wine, beer, or hard liquor. If your idea is to conserve money by drinking cheap booze, so you can have more cheap booze, you're already in trouble.

Rule #37
Never get carried away drinking alcoholic beverages which taste non-toxic. Fruity drinks with umbrellas in them, flavored alcohol and wine coolers are the most common culprits. These drinks often mask the taste of alcohol and

you will end up drinking far more than you should and eventually, throwing-up or maybe something even worse.

Rule #38
If your stomach and your mind cannot handle hard liquor, don't drink it. Trying to cover up your inability to hold your liquor through drinking fruity drinks, light beer, or wine-coolers is sissy and setting yourself up for a drunken disaster. Just say "no thank you" and drink water.

Rule #39
Never take photos of yourself naked. Never. No questions.

Rule #40
Never take video of yourself naked. Never!

Rule #41
Think long and hard before getting a tattoo. They are permanent and they do not age well. The only exception to this rule is if you are absolutely sure you have a phrase or a symbol that means something dear to you, such as the Olympic Rings and you're an Olympian. Having your boyfriend's name tattooed across your back is a very, very bad idea. The boyfriend may not be permanent but the tattoo will be.

Rule #42
Ears are generally the only place on your body, which are acceptable to pierce. Other areas are questionable and plenty of thought should go into this decision.

A GIRL'S RULES FOR LIFE, PLUS A GOLDEN RULE

Rule #43
Think twice before you pierce your face, meaning: eyebrows, lips, cheeks, nose, etcetera. I know of very, very, few, adult women who can actually pull this look off. Some women look absolutely lovely with facial piercings, but make sure you're one of them before moving forward. It isn't easy to go back once it's done.

Rule #44
I feel fairly safe in saying that there isn't a single 60+ year-old woman with a belly button piercing that actually looks good. No belly button piercing.

Rule #45
Good men do not take money from women. Ever. If your male significant other wants to take your money tell him to take a hike.

Rule #46
If you are seeing red flags with anything; boyfriends, girlfriends, buying a car, buying a house, etc. run, screaming down the street, as fast as you can. Your intuition is powerful and almost always 100% correct.

Rule #47
Past behavior is indicative of future behavior. Always.

Rule #48
Never stop and stand still in a doorway. Get in, get out, get on with your life.

Rule #49
Drive a big car or truck when you are young and a lousy, inexperienced driver. Save the zippy, expensive sports car for when you know what you are doing.

Rule #50
Always dump a significant other who tells you what to eat and how to dress.

Rule #51
Never bully anyone. The old saying, "if you can't say something nice, don't say anything at all," is true and real!

Rule #52
Be athletic! Ski, play golf, tennis, soccer, work out regularly, whatever works for you…just be athletic.

Rule #53
Do not settle for second best, ever. Get the A, not the B+. The same is true with partners. Do not settle for the person who is "just okay." You will be dissatisfied and unhappy through out the entire relationship.

Rule #54
Do not ever use drugs; pot, cocaine, crack, meth, heroine, pills, whatever. They destroy your brain and mess up your ability to make wise choices. If you take drugs, you will do stupid stuff. People who use drugs do stupid stuff all the time and end up in jail or dead. Don't do stupid stuff.

Unfortunately, the high that drugs provide is short. The low is long and very low. Besides, drugs make you ugly and give you bad breath.

Rule #55
Learn how to defend yourself. Learn a couple judo defense moves or other martial art moves. This will be a very valuable skill if you ever need it, lifesaving, quite frankly.

Rule #56
Most friends on social media are not friends. If you actually know them, then, at best, they're associates. If you don't know them, they're strangers. Friends are people you talk on the phone with and share experiences with. Friends are not equal to "likes" on a post.

Rule #57
Actually listen, don't simply hear. Speak WITH people, not TO them.

Rule #58
Never spill your beverage. Ever. If you knock over your drink on the dining room table, it is not an accident, it is you being careless. Do not be careless.

Rule #59
Never yell unless you really, really mean it. Yelling is a wasted activity way too many people use way too loosely. No one ever listens to a yeller. Most people tune yellers out entirely. Don't be a yeller.

Rule #60
Read. Read the newspaper. Read novels. Read fiction and non-fiction. Just get in the habit of reading. It exercises the brain and it is amazing how much you will learn!

Rule #61
Get good grades. At least carry a 3.0. Good grades show commitment and drive. Bad grades represent laziness and lack of caring. No one has ever been interested in someone who doesn't care about anything. Especially themselves.

Rule #62
Be passionate. Commit yourself to what you love and strive to be a pro. Study, practice, learn, implement, and succeed.

Rule #63
Always behave like a maker – not a taker. No one respects a person who does nothing but siphon off the public's dollar or a friend's hard-earned paycheck.

Rule #64
Drama is for the theater. Leave it there. No one likes a drama queen.

Rule #65
Don't be a sucker. Never fall for the sob story or a pity party. Generally, people who are in real, honest turmoil do not talk too much about it.

A GIRL'S RULES FOR LIFE, PLUS A GOLDEN RULE

Rule #66
Never feel impressed by people who appear to have a lot of money. Having money is easy to fake. Most people fake it. The truth is, only 1% of the population of the United States are actually considered wealthy. That's not too many.

Rule #67
Always live within your means. I don't care if you make $1,000,000 a year, live like you make half that.

Rule #68
Always say "excuse me." Even if you belch in private, say it.

Rule #69
Travel. You will learn more from traveling around the country and the world than from almost anything else.

Rule #70
Always act understated and tasteful. If you're not sure if you're following this rule, revisit your situation and make an educated choice.

Rule #71
If you chew gum, close your mouth. No one wants to see your molars.

Rule #72
Don't ever complain. If you have a problem or an issue,

find a solution and fix it. There is always someone who has it worse off than you do. Complaining never fixed anything and no one wants to listen to you.

Rule #73
Give advice only when you are asked for it. People very rarely act on or listen to unsolicited advice. In fact, offering up your advice to someone who hasn't asked for it will probably decrease your popularity rating, rapidly.

Rule #74
Always encourage others to succeed. Never tell someone they can't do something. Of course they can. Who are you to tell them otherwise? Be supportive.

Rule #75
Always come up with your own opinion. Never base your opinion on something someone else said! Get to the bottom of it and come to your own conclusions.

Rule #76
Don't ever follow the ordinary. Be a leader. Don't copy others. Don't mimic others. Don't fanaticize about being like someone else. Lead! Be a leader! Be yourself and be unique!

Rule #77
Find spirituality. You don't have to be a part of a structured religion, just find spirituality and practice it. Be mindful and conscious. Be aware.

A GIRL'S RULES FOR LIFE, PLUS A GOLDEN RULE

Rule #78
If your home allows for it, get a pet. Bring home a dog, a cat, a hamster, a fish, whatever. Get a pet that you need to be responsible for. Being responsible for a living creature other than yourself is well worth the trouble. You will grow and expand mentally and emotionally. Be wary of people who don't like pets.

Rule #79
Never take the "walk of shame." If you make a promise to yourself to not sleep around, you will never have to worry about this rule. If you are not aware of what the walk of shame is, basically it's when you've just had a one night stand, your hair is a mess, your make-up is smeared, you're still wearing the clothes you were in the night before (albeit somewhat disheveled) and you are caught walking through the living room, courtyard or front porch of the guy's house you just spent the night at...by his roomies and friends. The boys usually have all kinds of 'nice and complimentary' things to say to you as you leave. The walk of shame is degrading, embarrassing, and will make you feel like trash. Avoid it like the plague.

Rule #80
Don't get drunk and you won't get hung-over.

Rule #81
Always keep things tidy and pick up after yourself. Put your clothes away. Mop your floor. Vacuum your carpet. Wash your dirty dishes. Do your laundry. Unless you don't

mind mice, cockroaches, and filth, being tidy and cleaning up after yourself is imperative for healthy living. Having a messy space equals having a messy mind. Clean it up.

Rule #82
Always think about the variety of potential outcomes to every significant decision. Every situation has an outcome, good and bad alike. Before you jump into something, consider all of the different outcomes and make the wise choice.

Rule #83
Always remember the first guy who tells you he loves you is lying. You'll probably be 13 or 14, maybe 15. He has one thing on his mind, sex and his first sexual experience. He figures that if he tells you he loves you, you'll give him what he wants. Don't be a sucker. He is not in love you, he is in love with your pants. He doesn't even know what love is yet. This is serious.

Rule #84
Don't be a gossip. Gossiping is a waste of time and serves absolutely no purpose in the grand scheme of things. Besides, no one really cares and this action will come back and bite you…you know where.

Rule #85
Thinking things through is never a waste of time. Think things through, always. You'll be glad you did.

Rule #86
Always make sure your campfire is dead-out.

Rule #87
Never get into the car with a drunk or impaired person. When they crash, you will be very injured or possibly even die. It doesn't matter if they are your best friend, your husband or your cousin, whatever…do not get into the car under any circumstances! Call a cab.

Rule #88
Always carry some cash, hidden somewhere. Take a $100 dollar bill, fold it up and stow it in a secret compartment in your wallet. You never know when you may be in desperate need of a little cash. This $100 is not for spending on stuff, it is only for emergencies. Be wise.

Rule #89
When you are a professional and out in the big world, always try to surround yourself with people who are more experienced than you. You will learn from them and benefit. Immensely!

Rule #90
Always, always, always question authority. This does not mean to be rude to the police if you get pulled over for speeding. This means not to believe everything that someone who is in a position of authority tells you.

Rule #91

If you are walking at night and think someone is following you, cross the street immediately. If they continue to follow you, lace your keys between your fingers and make a fist around them. Then run like hell, screaming. The laced keys are just in case you need some kind of weapon. Priority number one is to get away as quickly as possible, however.

Rule #92

Eat ice cream periodically, or have a desert. If you must, you can substitute frozen yogurt in ice cream's place. Nonetheless, have a sweet once in a while.

Rule #93

Always get your car keys out of your purse before you leave the safety of a building. Never stand outside your car hunting and digging around in your purse for your keys, especially at night.

Rule #94

Don't sit in your car in a parking lot, ever. Don't check texts or emails, balance your checkbook, apply make-up, or whatever. No. Sitting in your non-running car is dangerous and you are an easy victim for a thief, car jacking or otherwise bad person.

Rule #95

Always trade up! Never trade down. This applies to everything; boyfriends, girlfriends, cars, houses, jobs, everything. By the way — selling a big house and buying a smaller house is not trading down. That's downsizing and it's different.

Rule #96
Do not wait for your retirement to spend money and have fun. You will die before you get there with this attitude. Be smart, and save money for retirement, but not every, single, extra penny. Take a vacation with your friends or family once in a while.

Rule #97
If you can't afford the best, then don't buy it until you can. Buying second rate and knock off items are cheaper but they are also often made in overseas sweatshops with child labor. Besides, they're junk and will fall apart. You'll end up buying two and spending more than you would have if you had just saved your money a little longer and purchased the real thing in the first place.

Rule #98
Practice conservation. Think about this one. How can you be more conservation conscious?

Rule #99
Know the difference between they're, there, and their and affect versus effect.

Rule #100
Always use spell check and proofread your documents.

Misspelled words are unacceptable in today's society and there is nothing worse than reading a document that has not been proofread and is loaded with mistakes and errors. Sloppy. That's all.

Rule #101
Know your wildlife and farm animals. Do not mistake a caribou for a deer or cows for bison. You will look like a fool among your ranch and outdoorsy friends. No one wants to look like a fool in front of a rancher, no one. Using the "I'm from the city" excuse is outdated and small minded.

Rule #102
Never say to yourself "my mom will never find out" because she will. Every time.

Rule #103
Always remember that in today's society "eyes" are everywhere. Everywhere! Small video cameras and webcams are placed on businesses, private homes, and even some street corners. So be careful of what you do in public. You may be caught on camera unintentionally.

Rule #104
Don't worry or care if someone doesn't like you. Throughout life there will be people who just don't like you. Who cares? This does not affect the kind of person you are. You are who you are and if they don't like you, for whatever reason, that's the way it is and it's their loss

anyway.

Rule #105
Never laugh at someone's name. Sure, some names are different and maybe even funny sounding but a name is the foundation of who a person is. Laughing at a person's name is nothing short of totally insulting.

Rule #106
You must learn to understand, accept and celebrate cultural diversity. Recognizing cultural diversity is not racism. Racism is hatred. Cultural diversity is the understanding that we are all culturally different and accepting that. Sorry sensitive people, but we are NOT all the same, we are all very, very different. And you know what, thank goodness for that!

Rule #107
Experience and appreciate food from different countries. Try Ethiopian food, Indian food, and Tai food among other options.

Rule #108
If you have a crabby, unfair, mean and hateful boss, find a new job. He or she will not change and you'll be spending a lot of your time at work. Don't waste your valuable time working for someone who upsets you. Find a job working with people you enjoy.

Rule #109
If you think the minimum wage is too low, get a college education.

Rule #110
Do not try to help people who will not help themselves, unless you are their psychiatrist and are required to. People must want to help themselves in order to succeed. You have absolutely zero control of whether or not someone wants to help themselves. This is a personal mindset.

Rule #111
Never listen to someone who tells you that you can't do something. Never. You can accomplish whatever you want to. Period.

Rule #112
If your significant other doesn't support your dreams and aspirations and only talks about their own, it's time to let that one go. Bye-bye. Relationships must be 100%/100%, not 50/50, not 60/40…etc. Each person must give 100%.

Rule #113
Never answer the door in a bathrobe or pj's. Never.

Rule #114
Do not be a guest who becomes a pest. Always consider staying in a hotel when you go to visit someone. If you feel comfortable staying in someone's home, don't wear out your welcome by staying for days on end. Keep the visit short

and sweet. They may invite you back.

Rule #115
Never open someone else's refrigerator or pantry looking for snacks or drinks. This is outright rude. Ask for something politely. Never help yourself unless you've been instructed to do so.

Rule #116
If you go to a home where there are shoes on the porch or just inside the front door, then the people who live there remove their shoes inside, so, you do the same! Many people feel that wearing shoes in their home is filthy. Just think about all the places the bottom of your shoes step in one day. Yuck.

Rule #117
Never, ever invite yourself! Ever! Rude beyond belief.

Rule #118
Do not park in other people's driveways. Always park on the street or in the guest parking area. Parking in someone's driveway and blocking what's in the garage (or what needs to go into the garage) is unacceptable car etiquette.

Rule #119
Learn how to shoot and handle a firearm properly. Know the different types of firearms: shotgun versus rifle, 9 millimeter pistols versus 40 caliber revolvers. I'm not saying run right out, buy a gun, and start packing heat, I'm saying

educate yourself. If you know the differences, and you know firearm procedures and laws, you will be much better off than the person who does not.

Rule #120
Start making up your bucket list before your turn 18. Get excited about places you'd like to visit and experience now. Why wait? If you haven't started your bucket list, get going.

Rule #121
Always remember that the future is not your friend. You cannot predict the future and you have no clue what it going to happen, in reality. So, don't get a false sense of security in thinking that the future is your friend, because it's not. The future will not protect you. Anything can happen to anyone at any time. Anything.

Rule #122
Never buy cheap shoes! Cheap shoes will hurt your feet, give you blisters and fall apart after one wearing. Quality shoes will not. If you are on a budget, buy quality shoes at the end of the season when they go on sale and save them for the following year. Styles don't change that drastically. Besides, if you're buying things that are so trendy that they'll be out of style the following year, you need to remember to be understated.

Rule #123
Never force your religious views on others. I invite you and

welcome you to have your own opinion and your own religious views. Always allow others that same luxury. Religion is interesting in that everyone thinks they are "right." It does not matter what faith you are, Christian, Muslim, LDS, whatever, your faith believes it is right. Your God is superior, your heaven is better and you're going to be saved. Truth is, no one REALLY knows who's right and who's not. No one will know until they're dead. Better check all the boxes.

Rule #124
Never feel bad about wanting to drive yourself somewhere. In fact, if you can, ALWAYS drive yourself. That way you can leave when you want to and you won't have to worry about the person who drove you, drinking or wanting to stay out until the wee hours. You can simply say goodnight or goodbye and be on your way, on your terms.

Rule #125
Never wear short-shorts (especially cut-off short-shorts) or tank-tops to church. No. Not ever.

Rule #126
If the wedding invitation is addressed solely to you, then you are the only person invited. Not you and your significant other. Don't bring your significant other.

Rule #127
Never tell someone what you want for your birthday or Holiday gift. Never. This tops the rude chart. In fact, it's a

great way to get nothing.

Rule #128
Never wear panty hose, stockings or tights with open toed shoes or sandals. No. In fact, avoid panty hose and stockings at all costs unless a situation really calls for it. Tights are okay in winter but NOT with open toed shoes or sandals. Never.

Rule #129
Keep your hands to yourself. Generally speaking, any significant other that's worth keeping, isn't going to be interested in keeping you if you're hanging all over them or overly physical with them. Nobody likes public displays of affection. Not the public and not the person you are with. The person you're with might not like it in private either. Be conscious. Don't hang on them like a cheap suit.

Rule #130
Don't advertise. If you are advertising you must have something to sell. Keep your boobs in your bra and keep your legs crossed or at least together. No one likes a crotch-shot, unless you're the paparazzi and are going to sell the photo of someone famous to the top tabloid magazine for $1,000,000. Oh, also, please keep your panties (whatever kind they may be) under your britches, not hanging out the top of your pants looking like a whale tail. This is kind of gross really.

Rule #131
Don't ever sit like a man.

Rule #132
Choose a college major that is flexible which you can actually do something with. Completing your degree is the most important thing, but try to choose an area of study that carries some weight in the real world. No one will be interested in you if you have a degree in basket weaving, unless you intend to be a pro basket weaver.

Rule #133
Always have a Plan B. Plan A is your first choice, of course, but go into everything with a Plan B in mind. There is a good chance you will need it.

Rule #134
Always have an escape route planned. Look around and know your surroundings. Look for the exits and know where they are. If there is a fire, a flood, the plane is going down or you're just on a really, bad, blind date that isn't working out, know your escape route 911.

Rule #135
Have a rescue-code phrase activated. Whether your savior is your mom, dad, sister, brother, neighbor or best friend, arrange with them a phase you both understand that means "save me." This will come in very handy if you are ever in a situation which you need out of ASAP. It can be activated verbally or through text. Of course, this 911 option in only

for non-emergent situations. Real emergencies still require the real 911.

Rule #136
Wear sunscreen. Even if you get tan, wear it. Skin cancer is gnarly and kills you, painfully. Sunscreen helps keep you safe from this hideous demise.

Rule #137
Never let anyone force you to attend a funeral, especially if its "open casket" and you don't feel comfortable with that. People are weird about death and often seem to feel better about it if they look at the person who died, dead and laying in the coffin. Other people prefer to remember the dead person "in-life." If you prefer the latter, than never feel pressure to go the viewing. Its' a personal choice, and I must warn you, the image of the dead person in the coffin will stay on your eyelids, forever.

Rule #138
Keep your politics close to your vest. People are very passionate about their political beliefs, some more than others, of course. It's usually a safe bet to keep your political views to yourself until you know someone well enough to share with them or you simply do not care if you piss someone off. Politics are generally not black and white, there is a whole lot of grey area there and people bounce around in the grey all over the place. If you decide to share, be prepared. You've been warned.

A GIRL'S RULES FOR LIFE, PLUS A GOLDEN RULE

Rule #139
Never waste your time and energy getting into an argument with a drunk person. Drunk people lack the ability to sensibly reason, after all, their brain has been somewhat tweaked by the effects of alcohol anyway. You are wasting your time. Besides, they won't even remember the argument, you'll be the one left with the memory and the scars.

Rule #140
If you make a promise, keep it. Never make a promise you don't intend to keep.

Rule #141
If someone is depending on you, come through. Be reliable.

Rule #142
Never feel envious or jealous of someone else. Being envious and/or jealous is useless. It serves absolutely no purpose and you just look bad and sound worse doing it.

Rule #143
If your intuition is telling you he doesn't love you, than he probably doesn't. There are many reasons for this phenomenon, no not the intuition part, the lying about loving you part. He may feel pressure from his mother to get a girlfriend, get married and have children. He may think he's "doing the right thing" by lying to you about his real feelings and hoping that someday he wakes up and actually does love you. (This will not happen). Or, he may be simply to chicken to tell you the truth. Whatever it is, get out

ASAP. If you stay in such a situation, you will end up wasting your life loving someone who does not love you back. This is worse than a torture chamber.

Rule #144

Always learn from your mistakes. We make mistakes every day. We say things we shouldn't or we go about something the wrong way. It's okay to make mistakes. Try to learn from those situations. Figure out how you could have done something differently and reached a better outcome. Just do not make the same mistake twice…or heaven forbid, three times.

Rule #145

Only you can make you happy. Love yourself and love yourself first! No significant other, retail purchase, home remodel or friend will make you happy if you are not happy with yourself to begin with. Becoming happy and building long term happiness are your responsibility and they come from within, not from external stimuli.

Rule #146

If you ever need a planned surgery, think ahead and set yourself up prior to the procedure. Stock your fridge with Gator-Aid, because you will be thirsty. Make up a week's worth of meals and put them in the freezer; simple stuff that you can just put in the microwave and eat. Bake up a loaf of banana bread to take your pills with. Move hazards out of the way, like area rugs, and set up a space where you will be comfortable…preferably close to the bathroom. Oh, *also have a barf bucket nearby as sometimes general anesthetic can make you sick to your stomach.*

Rule #147
If his mother doesn't like you now, chances are, she will never like you. You can make her cookies all you want, but the reality of it is, boy's mothers are very particular about the girls their son's hang out with. If you do not qualify in her eyes now, chances are very strong that you never will. Yes, this is unfair and maybe you never did anything wrong, but none-the-less, it is true.

Rule #148
Gambling is a waste of money. Don't gamble. Sure, going to Vegas is fun, friend-filled, weekend trip with overwhelming opportunities to break all the rules. Great! Just don't end up broke or you'll never make it home. Gambling is a great way to go broke, fast!

Rule #149
This should be an obvious one but I'll throw it in anyway, just in case. Be very wary of 45 plus year old bachelors. You probably know him already, Mr. "No, I've never been married." Also, beware of men who have been married more than twice. There's a plethora of reasons why the bachelor is still a bachelor (and no, one of them isn't because he just hasn't met Ms. Right yet) and there are two+ equally good reasons why the divorcee is divorced. Don't be mistake number three.

Rule #150
Talk less about yourself and listen more to others. People love to talk about themselves. For hours. No one really likes to listen to someone go on and on about themselves, but, better someone else do it than you. Don't let this be you.

Rule #151
If you do not understand something do not pretend that you do. Be honest and ask for an explanation. Nobody will ever mind giving an explanation, people will mind if you try to fake understanding something and end up saying something stupid. Then you just look like an idiot.

Rule #152
If you want to be treated respectfully, then you need to treat people respectfully. It is so easy to treat people respectfully. This requires no special skill and no special training. Just be thoughtful. In actuality, it is much harder to be disrespectful. You really have to plan and think that through. Being respectful should just roll off your tongue gently. Unless of course you are just a mean spirited person. In that case, people should treat you disrespectfully anyway. No one likes a bully.

Rule #153
Smile! You will get farther in life with a smile on your face than you will with a frown.

Rule #154
Never cheat! Cheating is for sloths. Don't be a sloth. Study,

prepare and succeed. If you do not study and you are not prepared, then face the consequences of making a bad choice. Do not be a sissy cheater. Yuck!

Rule #155
Never refer to an activity as "crap." Example: "Oh, no, I'm not into that crap." Why? Because the person you just said that to is very into "that crap" and you just totally insulted them, badly. If someone asks you if you participate in one activity or another and you don't, simply say, "No, I don't," politely.

Rule #156
If you assume, you will make an ass out of you and me (ass-u-me). Never assume anything and if you make a mistake and do assume something, admit it. The odds of you assuming correctly are stacked against you. This is just the way it is. So assume nothing.

Rule #157
You are not just a body, don't ever let anyone treat you like you are. You are a person, with feelings, thoughts, smarts and dreams. You are a mind and a soul. If someone is going to treat you like you're just an object of their lusts, give them the shoe. They deserve nothing.

Rule #158
Never fall in love with the front man for a band or a professional athlete. No. These people usually have huge egos, they're always on the road and every woman wants

them. This is a classic recipe for heartache and disaster and very, very rarely does it end well. Periodically these relationships turn out to be great, but generally speaking, this rarely happens.

Rule #159
Never subject yourself to unnecessary criticism or put downs. If your significant other is constantly pointing out your flaws and trying to "change" you, drop them like a hot potato. Nobody is perfect, nobody, not even them. Even though they often think they are flawless, they are not. If someone isn't going to accept you for who you are, flaws and all, they have no business taking up space in your life. After all, it is YOUR life.

Rule #160
If you are tired in the middle of the day, take a nap. There is absolutely nothing wrong with taking naps. You are not lazy, you are not sick and there is nothing wrong with you. You probably just need a little extra sleep. Do not feel guilty about laying down on your day off and taking a little snooze. If you feel like you need it, then you probably do.

Rule #161
Do not have the morals of an ally cat. Pride yourself on being moralistic and having a moral compass. Morals are powerful tools, which will protect you from disaster. If you behave in a morally responsible fashion, you will never feel guilty.

A GIRL'S RULES FOR LIFE, PLUS A GOLDEN RULE

Rule #162
If your significant other hates your friends and your friends hate your significant other, lose the significant other.

Rule #163
Practice safe sex, always. I cannot stress this one enough. If you are going to have sex, protect yourself, your health and your body. Some sexually transmitted diseases, like herpes, are permanent…as in never go away. HIV (AIDS) is also sexually transmitted and this one kills you. Just imagine for a minute meeting the partner of your dreams and having to say "Oh, by the way, I have herpes." Huh? Use a condom. It's easy, cheap and lifesaving.

Rule #164
Hating something or someone takes an enormous amount of energy. Don't hate things or people. If you simply don't like broccoli, then don't eat it. If you don't like someone, don't engage with them. Hating things is a total waste of time and energy. Just move on.

Rule #165
Always treat other people's property with respect and as well as you would treat your own. If you borrow someone else's clothes, take good care of them. Have them laundered before you return them. If you borrow someone else's car, drive safely. This is obvious stuff. However, if someone borrows your property and wrecks it, ruins it or returns it in foul condition, remove their contact information from your phone. This one's a zero.

Rule #166
There is never anything wrong with saying "No thank you." If you do not like the food choices – or you have dietary restrictions – at someone's home, simply say "no thank you." Do not inspect the food, you will insult the host. Wait and eat your food when you get home if you have an issue.

Rule #167
Never expect people to make special accommodations for you. Most often, if you have a special need or requirement, people will go out of their way and bend over backwards to be conscious of this and assist you. However, never EXPECT someone to do so. Never expect the restaurant to make you special food, never expect your host to stock their fridge with stuff just for you and never make demands of such. If you have a special requirement, plan ahead and stop at the store on your way to your accommodations or ask the restaurant in advance if they are able to meet your dietary needs.

Rule #168
If you are uncomfortable on a date, go Dutch. The two best ways to get out of that icky feeling of a bad date is to 1.) Pay for your own portion of the bill, and 2.) Drive yourself so you can leave when you want to.

Rule #169
Never brag about yourself. Nobody cares if your parents are wealthy. Nobody cares how big your diamond is, nobody

cares what you drive or how good you are at a certain sport, and nobody cares where you went to college (except your employer). You are not better than the next guy because you have stuff. Bragging is an ugly habit to get into and will not make you many friends.

Rule #170
Find some space and plant a garden. If all you have room for is an inside herb garden, that is fine, plant a garden. Grow things, water and harvest. You will gain a huge feeling of accomplishment as you use your own, fresh herbs in a salad or you chop your own carrots for a yummy, side dish. Well worth the energy and commitment.

Rule #171
Do not stay out past midnight. Give yourself a 12:00AM curfew and stick with it. Nothing good happens after midnight. Plenty of bad happens after midnight. Don't be a part of the bad.

Rule #172
Never run from a Grizzly Bear. Grizzly Bears can run up to 30 miles per hour. That's considerably faster than you can run. Hence, the bear will chase you down and maul you. Experts say to play dead instead. No real guarantees on survival, but evidently you may have a better chance of it if you go with the playing dead option.

Rule #173
Never pretend that you know how to ride a horse if you

actually do not. This is a disaster in the making. Always be honest with your horsey friends and if you don't ride, or if you haven't ridden since you were 10 years old, say so. Your friends will be happy to help you through the ins and outs of horseback riding. They will not be happy if you fall off, hurt yourself, and spook the horse because you lied.

Rule #174
If you're invited to someone's home for dinner, a party, or a short stay, bring something for your hosts! Never show up empty handed.

Rule #175
Always, always, always send thank you notes. It doesn't matter if someone sent you a silly, cheapo, little doo-dad gift or a Cartier watch. What matters is the fact that they took the time to find it, buy it, and send it to you. Which means they were thinking of you. Show them the same respect and send them a nice, little, thank you note. It takes very little time and it carries a lot of weight.

Rule #176
Be appreciative and gracious. In reality, no one needs to do anything for you. People might WANT to help you out from time to time, but no one NEEDS to and no one HAS to. If you are fortunate enough to have people who extend a helping hand to you, be appreciative! There is nothing worse than helping someone – even if it's something as little as buying them dinner – and they end up acting as though they deserved it. Don't be that guy.

A GIRL'S RULES FOR LIFE, PLUS A GOLDEN RULE

Rule #177
You do not EAT gum, you CHEW it. If you're eating it, you're doing it wrong.

Rule #178
Loaning a family member money is actually not a loan, it's a gift. You will not get that money back, so don't expect to. Hey, just the way it is.

Rule #179
Never behave in a vindictive manner. You will not always get your way. You will have your heart broken and friends will betray you. That's just part of life. However, always resist the urge to retaliate. Karma will get those who have harmed or wronged you. It's only a matter of time. Trust me. You need not do anything accept move on. Leave it all to Karma.

Rule #180
Never fall for the preverbal end-of-the-world scare tactic. Never. In 1999, thousands upon thousands of Americans became intensely anxious over the new millennium, the year 2000. At that time, the coming year was dubbed Y2K by the media and people thought all hell was going to break loose. People purchased expensive, power generators, canned food and non-perishables, weapons, gallons upon gallons of bottled water and so on. Guess what? Nothing happened. January 1, 2000 was exactly the same as December 31, 1999. The sun came up and the sun went down. I was there, I know.

Rule #181

When referring to a gaping gash in the side of a mountain, which climbers periodically fall to their deaths in, the word is pronounced "cre-voss." It is a word with French origin and is spelled, crevasse. Some people pronounce this word "crevis"...that's actually a crack in the sidewalk. Obviously, there is an entirely significant difference.

Rule #182

If you are ever invited onto your friend's yacht, learn the proper boating terminology and etiquette before you go. You may be asked to assist with lines (ropes) or to fetch something from below. Be prepared. When facing forward, the left side of the boat is the PORT side. The right side of the boat is the STARBOARD side. The bathroom is referred to as the HEAD. There's more. Learn it. There are rules, which go along with boating. Know them prior to boarding a friend's yacht. Do not look like a nautical fool around your mariner friends. Oh, and dress appropriately. Do not wear stilettos. Buy Top Siders if you do not have a pair.

Rule #183

Never flush a maxi-pad down the toilet.

Rule #184

Never carry your skis over your shoulder in a crowd. This is obvious. Chances are high that you will knock someone in the head. At the very least, you will piss them off. You may actually hurt them too. If you do not know how to carry your skis vertically, by the binding, ask someone who knows for a demonstration before you hurt someone.

Rule #185
Always shower and brush your teeth before you get onto an airplane. There is nothing more offensive than being forced to sit next to a person, on a flight, who has body odor and hideous breath. Especially, if that flight is hours long. Be courteous. It's a small space.

Rule #186
Never trespass on private property, especially in rural areas. Trespassing on private property is a great way to get shot. People who own large pieces of property along rivers or bordering public land typically do not take very kindly to folks traipsing through their private land to access the river or the public land on the other side. Oddly, often times if you kindly ask permission, they will grant it, but if you somehow think it is your human right to cross their land without permission, it's not. If you choose to do this, wear a bulletproof vest.

Rule #187
Always close the gate behind you.

Rule #188
If you are a gym rat, always wash your hands before you come home, and definitely before you put your fingers in your mouth. If you are a nail or a cuticle biter and go to the gym, you really, really need to wash your hands well when you are done with your work out. If you do not, you will

catch every strain of flu that comes through your town. If you keep your hands out of your mouth, wash them anyway or you will bring all those gym germs home to your family. Your family does not want them.

Rule #189
Never give someone a gift that they regularly purchase for themselves. If you are going to spend the money, take the time to think about a creative and unique gift. Get them something they will NOT buy for themselves. It's much more meaningful and memorable and the recipient will appreciate the thought you put into it immensely.

Rule #190
Take out your trash every day. Go around to each wastebasket in your home and empty it into a larger trash sack. Then take it out. No one wants rotting trash sitting in their home for days on end. This is just gross.

Rule #191
If you sprinkle when you tinkle, be a sweetie and wipe the seaty. (I can't take credit for this little poem, as I once read it on a bathroom wall, but it makes sense, doesn't it?)

Rule #192
Throwing money at a bad situation will not make it better. It does not matter how successful you are, if you simply throw money at your problems, they will not go away...in fact, they may get worse. You must give of yourself. Give emotional support, be kind, be understanding. Giving

yourself through offering your time and your patience is far more valuable than giving money. Money really isn't worth much in the emotional realm of things.

Rule #193
Don't make useless excuses. If you fail, you've failed. Accept it. Figure out why and fix it. Do not make foolish excuses as to why you failed. No one really cares anyway. You'll just sound ridiculous blaming other things or worse yet, other people, when everyone already knows it was really just your fault.

Rule #194
If you are behaving, you will never have to justify or explain your actions.

Rule #195
Purge annually. Go through your closet(s) and take a good look at the stuff you have stored in your garage. Get rid of the things you are not using and have no plans to use again. There is no good reason to cart all that stuff around with you. If you're not using it, then it's collecting dust and has become clutter. Give it away. Let someone else benefit from it. You'll clear your mind when you clear your space.

Rule #196
Do not become a pro-procrastinator. Get things done on time or before the deadline. This will make for far less stress on you, no question.

Rule #197
You cannot bullshit a bullshitter. Ever. Your mother or father may, in fact, be bullshitters. So there you go.

Rule #198
The only person you should compete against is yourself. Wasting your time and energy competing against others is simply that, a waste of time and energy. Who cares how others perform? Only care about how YOU perform. You're the only one that matters to you...not others. Do not measure your existence and performance against others. Measure your performance by your own standards.

Rule #199
If you think you stink at something then you will. You can only improve in areas that you encourage yourself to improve in. If you tell yourself that you can't do something, then, well, you can't. Don't tell yourself that you stink. Get out there and try to improve on a skill, which needs improving. If you are only able to draw stick figures, then take a drawing class and learn how to draw properly. You'll be mastering the skills in no time. You are perfectly capable.

Rule #200
Always get to the point. If you want something, ask for it. Don't beat around the bush with a bunch of smoke and mirrors. If you think the answer will be no, than it probably will be, but don't waste everyone's time with the verbal circling garbage. It's totally transparent. Everyone

can see through your song and dance.

Rule #201
If your parents are supporting you, whether you're a minor or an adult, everything belongs to them. If they are paying your phone bill, or your car payment, whatever, those items belong to your parents and your parents have the power and the right to take them from you if need be. When you're paying for your own expenses, then you have the power to take your car away from yourself…if necessary.

Rule #202
Do not be a sympathy hog. Bad things happen to good people. It's called life. Everyone has something bad happen in their life. Be kind and sympathetic during those times and people will return the favor to you when it is your time for tragedy. However, get on with your life. Do not expect people to continue feeling sorry for you for years after years. Feel the pain, recognize the mourning process and move on.

Rule #203
Always remember that your problems are not special. Everyone has problems. You may think your problems are worse than other's problems or harder to deal with than other people's problems but they are not. Simple as that.

Rule #204
Learn how to swim. You must know how to swim if you ever plan to be around any type of body of water; pool, lake, ocean, river, whatever. You need to know how to

survive in the water and better yet, possibly help someone who may not.

Rule #205
Your parents know what they are talking about, your friends and associates do not. When your friend tries to tell you that you can't get pregnant if you have sex while you're on your period, but your mom tells you otherwise, I've got news for you, your mother is correct. You can, absolutely, get pregnant while on your period.

Rule #206
Be conscious about your health and weight, but don't be obsessive about it. Be reasonable. If you eat good, healthy food and you are active you will not have to be weight conscious because your body will most often take care of itself. If you eat a bunch of junk food and do nothing but sit around, you will gain weight and be unhappy about it. Being healthy is well worth the exercise and healthy diet commitment. You will feel 100% better about yourself. There is a fine line though between being reasonable and being obsessive about health and weight. Be aware of your mindset.

Rule #207
Contrary to popular teenage belief, the best way to not get pregnant is to not have sex.

Rule #208
When you are in an elevator, always stand closest to the

control panel. Realistically, you cannot get out of the elevator every time a "stranger" gets in...what you can do is always stand by the control panel so you can hit the alarm button or grab the emergency phone if you need to.

Rule #209
Never go out on a boat or on a water toy with someone who has been drinking or may be under the influence of something impairing. Deep water, machines with spinning propellers, and humans on alcohol or drugs NEVER mix well. This is a recipe for disaster and will end badly.

Rule #210
When out in the country or wilderness, make sure you know the difference between a pit viper – or venomous, potentially deadly snake – and a harmless snake. There are distinct, recognizable makings on deadly snakes and their heads are shaped like an arrowhead. Obviously, the rattlesnake usually rattles...but not always. Before your trip, take some time and look at photos of the different snake species in the geographic region where you are visiting. Don't make the mistake of confusing a venomous snake with a harmless snake. It could be a very costly mistake.

Rule #211
There are mistakes you can forgive but you mustn't forget. Forgiving someone for doing something that you didn't approve of or appreciate is one thing, forgetting that they did it, is another. I highly suggest you not FORGET what

they did (if that's even possible). Remember, past behavior is indicative of future behavior. Don't put yourself in the same predicament twice.

Rule #212
You will not get ahead by trying to be a "people pleaser." In fact, this behavior may put you at a disadvantage. Stand up for what you believe in, whether or not the person you're speaking with agrees with your opinion. Trying to tell people what they want to hear or always agreeing with people, especially if you really don't, is basically spineless and cheating no one but yourself.

Rule #213
If you are truly injured, seek medical attention. If you're simply hurt, put a band-aide on and get going.

Rule #214
Don't carry on and on about your health issues or your injuries. No one really cares if you have lower back pain, a knee injury, headaches, whatever. Of course, those close to you certainly do have a general concern for your health and wellness, but that's really it. Plus, if you're constantly complaining about your aches and pains, when you really get hurt…you may get ignored.

Rule #215
Do not give money to people standing on the street corners with cardboard signs of angst. Otherwise known as panhandlers. The odds are high that these people are addicts

of some sort and will just take the money you give them to buy more drugs and/or alcohol. Study after study has shown this to be true. If you'd like to help, please give to your local shelter. The local shelter is the best place to help the folks who are in need.

Rule #216
Use your manners! Say "please" and "thank you." Remember to use "bless you" when someone sneezes and always wait to begin eating until everyone at the table has been served. There's more. This is just a small smattering of life's necessary "manners." If you do not know your manners, learn them. The time will come when they will be very beneficial and handy to you. I promise.

Rule #217
Never act "star-struck." Seeing a celebrity or a famous athlete in person can be exciting, but you certainly need not drool on yourself over it. Don't scream, don't wiggle all around, don't stare, don't ogle, just go on about your business. Some famous people are approachable and some are not. Use your intuition.

Rule #218
Ball equals child (or dog). Every time. When a soccer ball, basketball, or ball of any kind rolls or bounces into the road, a child (or dog) will promptly follow. Don't hit the child with your vehicle. When you see that ball roll into the road, stop your car immediately. Wait. After the child fetches their ball, you may proceed…slowly. This is a really

good reason why NOT to speed in neighborhoods.

Rule #219
Animals have souls! Anyone who tells you otherwise doesn't have a soul themselves. Dogs smile, cats sneer, wildlife never ceases to amaze with their "human-like" behaviors. Be kind to animals, all of them. Be very, very wary of people who are mean to animals.

Rule #220
Throughout your life, people will continually try to rip you off. Whether your car needs new brakes or you need a plumber, whatever, beware! Ask a lot of questions, especially if you do not understand what's being done and/or why. Always ask for a written estimate as to the ensuing charges. Remember, it's your money.

Rule #221
Go to the museum. Art museum, history museum, science museum, any museum, just go. You will learn things you did not know before and you will feel good about that. When you are on your travels, look into the local museum(s) and pay it a visit.

Rule #222
Be articulate. Be eloquent. Speak clearly and intellectually. It does not matter what your background is. It doesn't matter if you have an accent of some sort. It doesn't matter what race or ethnicity you consider yourself. What matters is that you verbally present yourself in a respectable

manner. People will listen, understand and appreciate what you have to say.

Rule #223
Money is (at the very least) 100 times easier to spend than it is to make. Be very careful with the money you've worked so hard to earn. Let's face it making good money can be a very arduous task. You must work at it. You must focus on it and you must commit yourself to it. People who are making "easy money" are probably doing something illegal, like selling drugs, or they're simply lying about how much they really make.

Rule #224
Try your best never to ever pass gas in public, but most certainly never pass gas in a crowd. This seems obvious but I am always amazed at the crazy people who do this! Sometimes passing gas can't be avoided but at least do your friends and yourself a favor and step away from the group. No one wants to be exposed to that…no one. And you know what, if you're older than five, it's not really funny either. Sorry.

Rule #225
Never drink water from a natural stream, river, creek or spring even if it looks crystal clear and clean. It's not. You'll get giardia and have diarrhea for weeks. Basically, you'll get really sick. No one wants giardia. It's nasty.

Rule #226
Nothing is free. Everything costs something or leaves you owing something to somebody. For example, drugs are always "free" the first time someone uses them, but they certainly aren't free in the long run, but rather very costly…in more ways than one. Remember, every time someone seemingly gives you something…payment, or payback, is coming. "No, thank you" can come in very handy here. Never be left owing someone something.

Rule #227
If you live in the USA, honor our Nation's service men and women, Army, Navy, Air Force, Marines, Coast Guard. You may not believe in war, and that is fine, but you must always appreciate that there are individuals; daughters, sons, husbands, wives, parents, who have laid their lives on the line and experienced the unthinkable so that you can have freedom! FREEDOM! Not clear on what the word freedom means? Look at photos of the Holocaust and how the Jews experienced organized genocide by Hitler and the Nazi Regime. Now, picture yourself experiencing the horrors of Auschwitz (the concentration camp). Did you shudder? Or, if you prefer something more modern-day, take a look at women in the middle east and picture yourself as a piece of "property," with not a single right. That should clarify the word freedom for you.

Rule #228
Life is not fair. I'm sure you've heard this phrase at lease one thousands times, unfortunately, it's true. You will not

always get your way. Men have always made more money than women and continue to do so. People are discriminated against for one thing or another all the time. The list goes on and on. This is just one of those things. You do not have to like this, but you do have to recognize it.

Rule #229
You are in charge of your own destiny! If you sit around and wait for things to happen for you, nothing will. If you go out and make things happen for yourself, than the sky's the limit. Get out there and shake things up.

Rule #230
Never post anything on social media that you're priest, grandparent, or FUTURE EMPLOYER will not approve of. The key words here are 'future employer.' There are piles and piles of hiring managers out there who will not even consider interviewing you if you've posted questionable photos or statements. Be smart about this. It's your professional career we're talking about and those internet posts never go away.

Rule #231
You are, in fact, mortal. You are not invincible despite what you may think. Bad things will happen to you just like they happened to that other guy down the street. You are not special nor do you have super powers. A good example of this is that if you shoot heroine, you WILL become addicted…this is not debatable. This rule is a good one to keep in mind if you're ever considering doing

something that will end badly. The issue is that it will, in fact, end badly, and you know it. Mental and physical injury or death is eminent. You don't want any of these options. All of these options are bad.

Rule #232
Never issue a permanent cure for a temporary problem. This rule can cover many topics but the most obvious is that of suicide. Suicide is permanent, there's no going back, there's no changing your mind. Permanent. Suicide is not a problem solver. It is not an option. Problems are temporary and always have solutions. If you are in so much mental pain that you feel you simply cannot go on, seek help! Immediately! There is help out there and it works. Your life is far too valuable to end. Period.

Rule #233
Never threaten anyone. Threats are very dangerous. If you threaten someone, then be prepared for a challenge. Then what are you going to do? Something illegal? No. Save yourself the trouble and just avoid threatening people all together.

Rule #234
If you are going to give someone (like a partner) an ultimatum, get ready and brace yourself. People do not typically respond well to ultimatums. In fact, ultimatums usually provide a person with a really easy way out. On the flip side, if you do give someone an ultimatum and they do respond in the predicted manner, consider yourself lucky.

You got rid of that one the easy way! Plus, you've tested their mettle and they failed. It was doomed from the get-go.

Rule #235
You will kiss a lot of frogs. Odds are very, very high that your first love will not be your life-long partner. This is a good thing because as you grow up you're wants and needs, in a mate, will change. There will be plenty of potentials, and also plenty of throw-backs. The moral to this story is that when your fist love breaks your heart, there is light at the end of the tunnel and you will recover. It will sting for a little bit but you'll be fine. I promise.

Rule #236
Your parents are not your servants. We are here to help, yes. We are here to at least feed you, clothe you, get you where you need to be, educate you, and LOVE you. We are NOT here to jump at your every whim, buy you your every wish, pay for your friend's movie tickets and snacks, act as a taxi cab for the entire 7th grade girl's class, and/or take your lunch to you when you've forgotten it on the counter. This list is somewhat limited…there's a lot more. We will often do these things out of the goodness of our hearts, but they are most certainly not requirements in our Parental Contract. If you've had one, or all, of these things done for you lately, consider yourself very, very fortunate and then get your act together.

Rule #237
If your parents say that he's a thug, loser, a-hole, jerk, etc.,

etc., he probably is. By now, your parents know their stuff and are also excellent judges of character...both with boys and girls. So, although you will not want to listen to them and you are absolutely sure they do not know what they are talking about, they do. You have two choices; give him the boot and save yourself now or hang out with him until he does something crummy and hurts your feelings tremendously, proving your parents correct. It's a given. Sorry. He is an a-hole.

Rule #238
When he (or she) breaks up with you, it REALLY isn't you! Really! I have avoided telling personal stories in this book but this particular rule requires one to make a point. Quite frankly, when I was young, I had my heart shattered when a boy broke up with me and I cried and cried. I wondered what on Earth I could do to make him like/love me. What did I do wrong? Why did he not want to be with me? I was cute, relatively smart, athletic...I mean, why? Did I not come from a "wealthy enough" family? Was my car not cool enough? I had no idea. I second-guessed myself left and right. It was torture. Truth is, it really was not me. He turned out to be gay. It was HIM! What a relief! I'm telling you, it's NOT YOU and it never is. Some boy or girl may "fall out of love" with you, or many never love you at all. It is not you! It is them and all of their own issues.

Rule #239
Good opportunities rarely present themselves more than once. Great opportunities almost always require some kind

of change and some level of risk. Think things through and then… take it!

Rule #240
Do not ever pick your nose while at a televised sporting event. You will end up on national TV… picking your nose. Awesome!

Rule #241
If someone is pointing a handgun at you, never grab the gun. You will end up pulling it toward yourself, which will actually cause the perpetrator to pull the trigger and shoot you, whether they were planning on it or not. Do whatever you have to do to just get away!

Rule #242
Never assume that just because you are traveling to visit their town, this automatically means you can stay with them ('them' being your friends, your family…). Unless you are specifically invited to stay with them, you are actually NOT invited to stay with them at all. Don't take this personally, just err on the side of caution and courtesy and get a hotel room.

Rule #243
If you choose to dress provocatively prepare yourself to be treated like a piece of meat. You see, what you may consider as fashion forward, cutting-edge couture, he may see as a neon sign screaming, "cheap and easy sex." Provocative clothing will solicit unwanted advances, every time. This

never fails! This is not an excuse to preach to you on how to dress. It is just the way it is. Oh and to add insult to injury, the person YOU may be interested in "impressing" with your fashionista ways will probably be nothing short of disgusted with your trashy style. Do yourself a favor and keep it tight.

Rule #244
Typically, business partnerships are a disaster in the making. Unless you are a partner in a law office, an accounting firm or a physician's office, having a business partnership with someone, especially family members, is trouble from the get-go. If you want to go into business for yourself, than do it BY yourself. You will have control and be able to make your own business decisions. This is a much better solution than having to ask your "partners" for permission every time you need to make an office supplies run. A great way to ruin a friendship or a marriage is to go into business together.

Rule #245
If a private, family matter is shared with you, by your mom, dad, sister, brother, etc. and you are asked to keep it to yourself, then for goodness sake, keep it to yourself! This is especially true if the information is about another living, family member. You have absolutely no idea the unnecessary damage and pain you can and will cause by opening up your mouth and blabbing the private details that were shared with you. Consider yourself fortunate to be informed and leave it at that.

Rule #246
Always walk with a purpose! Stand tall, walk swiftly, head-up and looking where you are going, especially at night. Never walk like a victim; head down, gaze glanced downward, slow gate. Walking like a victim is asking to be a victim.

Rule #247
You can absolutely get a bad reputation by the ole "guilty by association" concept. Hanging out with those who really do have solid reasons to carry a bad reputation will bring you the same fate. Choose your team wisely.

Rule #248
The day will come when you do not make the team, the cheerleading squad, the cut in general, don't freak out, life goes on. You will be amazed by what opportunities present themselves to you. You may think that all of your skills and your whole life was based on making the soccer team but you didn't make it... Trust me, your whole life was NOT based on that one event. Your whole life will be based on zillions of events. Make the next one yours! Make the next one count!

Rule #249
If you experience road rage from another driver, stay in your car and just go on about your business. NEVER get out of your car and confront the raging person, never! You just don't know what that angry person is capable of. It may be nothing serious and just a bunch of name-calling

and bird flipping, or he/she could have a gun under their seat just waiting to be pulled out, pointed at you and fired. Don't be at the wrong end of that crazy person's cross hairs. Just drive on and forget about it. I know, it's easier said than done... but just do it. You'll be better off for it.

Rule #250
Do not apologize unless you mean it. Simply blurting out a sloppy "I'm sorry" means nothing. Actually FEELING bad and feeling sorry for doing something crummy is what matters. If you don't feel bad and sorry then don't apologize. Everyone knows you are not really sorry anyway. Be genuine.

Rule #251
Social media is the preverbal bathroom wall of the 21st Century. In the "olden days," girls who did naughty things, or were accused of doing naughty things, often discovered their name and their so-called offence written on the inside of the girl's bathroom stall, example: Sally Jones is a slut! Humiliating to say the least. However, the only people who saw the scribble were other girls and the janitor. Social media's reach is just a little more expansive. Always be aware of this as the more active you are on social media and the bigger presence you make of yourself, the higher your odds are of being a scribble. You're too good to be reduced to a scribble.

Rule #252
Never fly fish or play golf in a thunder storm. This seems

obvious but every, single year someone does this and invariably gets struck by lightning. Getting struck by lightning will ruin your day and possibly kill you. That would be bad.

Rule #253
Do not be a know-it-all. Nobody likes a know-it-all. Generally, know-it-all's actually do not know-it-all and only end up insulting everyone else's intelligence. Know-it-all's are annoying as hell and make people clench their jaws and squeeze their fingers into fists.

Rule #254
There are two kinds of funny; funny-strange and funny-haha. Being funny-haha is okay as long as you don't stretch it too far and end up being funny-strange. People who are funny-strange make other people roll their eyes and want to get away. Don't be that girl who everybody wants to get away from.

Rule #255
Believe what you want to believe but never force your beliefs on others. This goes along with the religion rule, obviously. You may be straight, you may be gay, or you may be bi. I do not care what you are. You need not care what others are either. It is none of your business whether Sally Jones in Georgia is gay and wants to marry her partner...no more than it is her business if you want to marry your partner. Look both ways. Always ask yourself, "How would I feel if some total stranger told me I couldn't do

something I felt was right for me, because of THEIR personal beliefs?" Just worry about yourself and apply your beliefs to yourself, not others. Wow, that's some crazy, out-there stuff.

Rule #256
Life is too short to sit through a boring movie.

Rule #257
When at a social event, dinner, lunch or any event where you are sharing time and space with others HANG UP YOUR PHONE! Be social with the folks you are with. Never sit at a table with other mates while talking on the phone to someone else. This is horrendous. I see it all the time and it still makes me cringe. If the call is that important, go outside.

Rule #258
Be proud of your accomplishments. Never, ever let anyone belittle what you have done in life. Everything you do is important.

Rule #259
Be a difference maker. If you think something needs to be changed or made better, make the change to make it better! There is no reason why you cannot be a person for change.

Rule #260
Be mysterious. You do not need to tell everyone everything about you. You don't need to tell your partner or BFF

every, last, gritty detail about yourself. Keeping things private and to yourself is totally respectable.

Rule #261
When staying in a hotel, remember there are others in the hotel, as well (unless it's a haunted, abandon hotel). Try your best to be courteous. No yelling, screaming or running in the hallway in the early morning or late at night. No jumping up and down on the beds or running in the rooms if you're higher than the first floor. You'll sound like a herd of elephants to the rooms below, awaken everyone and end up getting scolded, or even asked to leave in the middle of the night. That would be bad.

Rule #262
Never fish in your own pond. Boys and girls in your own pond are off limits. Think this through. Think of the aftermath if the relationship fails, which it probably will. You will have to see that person day in and day out. You'll be sitting in the same classroom, riding on the same bus, eating in the same lunch area. You may even have PE with that person. This sounds dreadfully uncomfortable.

Rule #263
If your parent buys a drug testing kit, then don't try or use drugs. You will get caught and you will most likely have to face some kind of consequence. The consequence will probably be far worse than the high you got from the drugs. Just steer clear of drugs. They only do harm.

Rule #264
When parking your car in a public parking space, take only one space. Chances are your car is not so great that you need to take up two spaces. If you are concerned about the well being of your vehicle, park it at the end of the line where there will be a concrete curb on one side of your car or the other. This is not foolproof, of course, but at least you know that one side of your car will be safe.

Rule #265
Make choices that positively affect your life. Do not make choices based on what others think will best enhance their lives. It's your life and your choices that matter.

Rule #266
Just because something is legal does not mean it's a good idea to use, eat, drink or do it. There are numbers of "legal" things that are dangerous and harmful. This is another really great opportunity to think things through and ponder the outcome prior to jumping in.

Rule # 267
In some cases, it's a good idea to grow a thicker skin. There will always be taunting, harassing, verbally abusing bullies out there. We have laws and rules to protect people against these annoying folks but prior to jumping into the legal system, make a conscious decision to not let this person get under your skin. See if that helps. Of course, if this person is threatening or you are afraid for your safety, call the police. Immediately.

A GIRL'S RULES FOR LIFE, PLUS A GOLDEN RULE

Rule #268
You have been your parent's life for the last several number of years. They have given you everything they are capable of giving. Some parents give more, some give less but most give all that they can. Be conscious of this. Be thoughtful of this. Make a wise choice because your parents would be devastated if you didn't. Show them you have been listening. They will be more proud of you than you can imagine.

Rule #269
Always, always shut the gate behind you. Friendly reminder.

Rule #270
Dating a rodeo cowboy can be a potentially disastrous scenario. Although they are often very handsome, they are also regularly injured and spend weeks on the road. So unless you feel like playing the caregiver and/or you don't mind being left alone for weeks at a time, this is a bad match for you. Unless, of course, you are a rodeo cowgirl, then you already know the drill.

Rule #271
Police are generally supposed to "protect and serve." They are not here to be your friend or listen to your sob story about why you were speeding or why you were breaking the law. If you get pulled over or questioned by the police, answer the questions and behave yourself. No matter how pretty or sexy you think you are, do not act like an ass hole

or you will end up in jail. While you're wasting the officer's time behaving poorly, someone else may be in desperate need of police help. Just do your best to try and stay out of trouble in the first place and this will never be an issue.

Rule #272
Be aware that motorcycles are indeed very dangerous. Especially if operated without wearing a helmet. Riding a motorcycle without a helmet is never a good idea. Wear the helmet. It may not save your life but then again, it might.

Rule #273
So many of the problems in society could be so easily solved with the use of sensibility. This is true in life, as well. Being sensible about things will keep you going down the correct road. When people become wrapped up and obsessive about issues they have no control over, they are clearly lacking sensibility. Be sensible.

Rule #274
Have direction. Schedule your day. Plan your year.

Rule #275
Get control of the sensitivity meter. There is such a thing as being too sensitive. It is one thing to have feelings, it is completely another to be overly sensitive about every little issue that comes along. Pick your battles and toughen up a bit.

A GIRL'S RULES FOR LIFE, PLUS A GOLDEN RULE

Rule #276
Carry a purse with a zipper closure, not a flimsy button or Velcro closure. We live in tough times where people will steal from you at the drop of a hat. If your wallet is within reach, they will take it. Never leave your purse unzipped and hanging open. Zip up your purse and keep what is yours.

Rule #277
If you are thinking about plastic surgery, do it for yourself. Do not do it for someone else. This is your body and plastic surgery is relatively permanent.

Rule #278
He (or she) will not love you more if you "change" for them. First, people do not change, they grow and morph but they generally do not change. Second, why should you change? Aren't you awesome just the way you are? Yes, yes you are! If he or she isn't going to love you for whom you are, then they are not for you.

Rule #279
Never engage in hand-to-hand combat with anyone who is bigger and stronger than you, if you can avoid it. Run like hell first. Only engage in combat if it is the last remaining option. There is a good chance you will be overpowered by a bigger and stronger person. Also, if you are smaller and lighter, you may be able to get away and run faster than a larger person. Hence, running is the better option.

Rule # 280
Try to avoid the temptation of using text slang, such as 'gonna' and 'kinda.' These are not real words and they are not found in the dictionary.

Rule # 281
You do not have to or need to like everyone you meet and come across. There is no rule that says we must like everyone. This is garbage. Pretending to like someone when you really don't is a waste of energy for you and totally unfair to the other person. You need not be rude, just keep to yourself.

Rule #282
Never expect your host or hostess to put their animals in a kennel or outside simply because you are coming to visit. The animals live there. That is their home. You are a guest. Please behave like one.

Rule #283
Prior to taking your clothing to the cleaners or donating it, make sure to check all of the pockets for items you may have forgotten, as well as money!

Rule #284
Always remember that your name is attached to everything you do. Treat your name with the respect it deserves and value it like your most prized possession. Your reputation does matter and your name deserves a good one.

A GIRL'S RULES FOR LIFE, PLUS A GOLDEN RULE

Rule #285

If your parent(s) suddenly stop asking questions, setting deadlines and curfews for you, and stop demanding certain behaviors of you, beware. You might want to perk up and make sure you make your next choices wisely. This is an ancient parent trick...it's called "give them enough rope and they will hang themselves." In other words, without the proper parental boundaries you will eventually do something really stupid...and get into trouble. The fact alone that I shared this trick with you is a no-no, so consider yourself fortunately informed and behave accordingly. Don't hang yourself.

Rule #286

Pay your bills and financial obligations on time. Maintaining your good credit is of upmost importance if you would like to maintain your financial individuality. Poor credit will leave you reliant on someone else's good credit. Kind of like being in financial jail.

Rule #287

If you are camping in the desert, shake out your shoes prior to putting them on. Sometimes, desert dwelling creatures will crawl into a shoe at night. Scorpions are notorious for this.

Golden Rule

We parents know you will have sex and lose your virginity at some point and most likely prior to you meeting your future life-partner. What we hope for is that you'll exercise excellent judgment with this major step, as there is no going back. You must be mature enough emotionally to handle this experience. You must be absolutely sure of yourself and confident in your decision. You must recognize that sex only makes things more complicated and weird. You must only partake in this action on YOUR OWN TERMS. Never, ever do it for HIM (or for her for that matter). Never assume that by having sex you will get married and live happily ever after OR save a seemingly doomed relationship. This is a crock and is totally make-believe stuff for the movies. It is not real, in the least. In reality, be prepared for the relationship to end shortly after your sexual encounter. Also, be prepared for your partner to talk, brag and tell his/her friends all about it. Frankly, this is most often how it works. Lastly, never assume that you can't get pregnant your first time, because you absolutely can. You must be 100% prepared and even if you think you are, you probably aren't. This is a really good opportunity to think things through…perhaps more than once.

Be well, young lady, be well.

A GIRL'S RULES FOR LIFE, PLUS A GOLDEN RULE

ABOUT THE AUTHOR

Stacie Davies is a published author and blogger who focuses much of her work on topics such as:, parenting and family matters, teen issues, lifestyle choices, and female subject matter.

More of her work can be found at her website: www.sd-writes.com

Made in the USA
San Bernardino, CA
07 October 2016